DONATED BY PTA

Z 216

from SEA TO SHINING SEA

WASHINGTON, D.C.

By Dennis Brindell Fradin

CONSULTANTS

Kathryn Collison Ray, M.S., M.A., District of Columbia Public Library

Robert L. Hillerich, Ph.D., Consultant, Pinellas County Schools, Florida;
Visiting Professor, University of South Florida

CHILDRENS PRESS®
CHICAGO

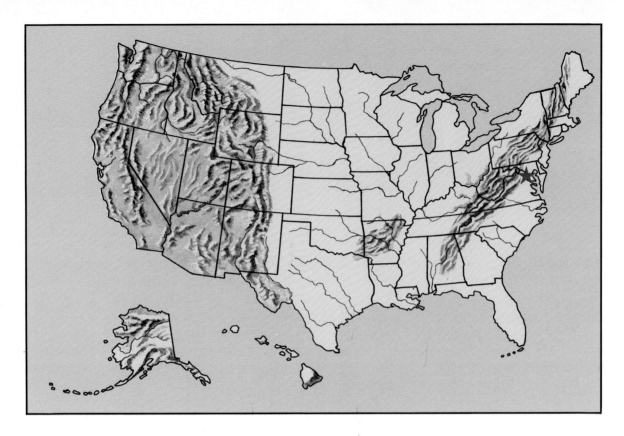

Washington, the District of Columbia, is the capital of the United States. The city lies on the Potomac River, between Maryland and Virginia.

For my nephew, David Philip Bloom, from Uncle Dennis with love

For its help, the author thanks the Historical Society of Washington, D.C.

Project Editor: Joan Downing
Design Director: Karen Kohn
Research Assistant: Judith Bloom Fradin
Typesetting: Graphic Connections, Inc.
Engraving: Liberty Photoengraving

THIRD PRINTING, 1993.

Library of Congress Cataloging-in-Publication Data

Fradin, Dennis B.
  Washington, D.C. / by Dennis Brindell Fradin.
    p. cm. — (From sea to shining sea)
  Includes index.
  Summary: An introduction to the nation's capital city, its history, people, and sites of interest.
  ISBN 0-516-03851-6
  1. Washington (D.C.)—Juvenile literature.
[1. Washington (D.C.)] I. Title. II. Series: Fradin, Dennis B. From sea to shining sea.
F194.3.F73   1992   91-32919
917.5304'4—dc20   CIP
                                   AC

Tourists at the Lincoln Memorial

Table of Contents

Washington, D.C., is the capital of the United States of America. The federal government has its headquarters there. It is also home to more than six hundred thousand people.

During the country's early years, eight cities served as the capital. Finally, in the 1790s, Washington, D.C., was built as the permanent capital. The city was named in honor of George Washington. He was the country's first president. D.C. stands for District of Columbia. Being a district means that the city is not part of any state.

Many famous landmarks stand in Washington, D.C. The White House is the home of the president and his family. In the Capitol, Congress meets and makes laws. The Washington Monument, the Jefferson Memorial, and the Lincoln Memorial honor three great presidents. Each year, millions of people visit these famous places.

The capital is known for other things as well. Where do giant pandas live? Where do the Redskins

A picture map of Washington, D.C.

play football? Where were Duke Ellington, Goldie Hawn, and J. Edgar Hoover born? The answer to these questions is: Washington, D.C.!

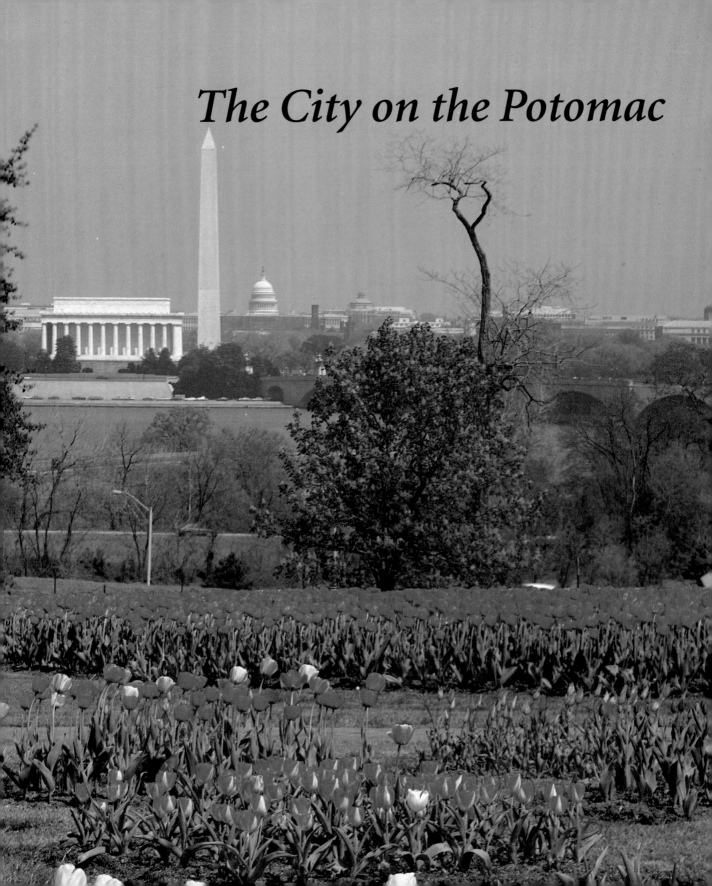

The City on the Potomac

THE CITY ON THE POTOMAC

Except on its southwestern edge, Washington, D.C., is diamond shaped. The corners of the diamond point north, east, and south. The city covers 69 square miles. It lies between Maryland and Virginia. Maryland borders the capital on every side but the southwest. There, the Potomac River forms the city's border with Virginia.

The Anacostia River flows south through the city's eastern part to the Potomac. Rock Creek runs north to south into the Potomac. It cuts through northwestern Washington.

Washington has four sections. They are the Northwest (NW), Northeast (NE), Southwest

Left: The four sections of Washington
Right: The Falls on the Potomac

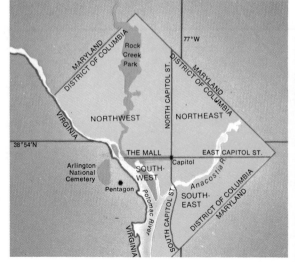

(SW), and Southeast (SE). These directions show a place's location in relation to the Capitol. The Capitol is near the center of the city. For example, the White House is at 1600 Pennsylvania Avenue, NW. This means that it is in the city's Northwest section. It is northwest of the Capitol.

CLIMATE, PLANTS, AND ANIMALS

Washington, D.C., is in the region of the country called the South. Like other southern cities, its climate is warm. January temperatures often top 45 degrees Fahrenheit. July temperatures often top 90 degrees Fahrenheit. Washington is also very humid. There is much moisture in the air. This makes some summer days quite uncomfortable.

Many kinds of trees and animals live in the city. The capital is famous for its lovely Japanese cherry trees. They were a gift from the mayor of Tokyo in 1912. Oaks, sycamores, and magnolias also beautify the city. Raccoons, squirrels, opossums, and even foxes can be seen in the capital's parks.

Mockingbirds, blue jays, thrushes, and Baltimore orioles fly about the city. President Theodore Roosevelt listed ninety kinds of birds that he could see from the White House.

Washington's Japanese cherry trees were planted around the Tidal Basin.

The wood thrush is the city's official bird.

9

From Ancient Times Until Today

Fossils of sea animals have been found around Washington. They show that many millions of years ago, inland seas covered the area. About 100 million years ago, dinosaurs roamed the region. Their fossils have also been found around the capital.

American Indians

People first reached the Washington area a few thousand years ago. They were ancient Indians who moved about while hunting and fishing. Later, the Piscataways were among the American Indian groups that lived in the region.

The Indians built villages that they surrounded with wooden fences. Indian women grew corn and beans in fields near their homes. Men fished with nets and hooks in the Potomac and Anacostia rivers. The men also hunted deer and wild turkeys with bows and arrows. Animals provided more than food. The skins were used to make clothing and moccasins. Sewing needles and fishing hooks were made from the animals' bones.

EXPLORERS AND TRADERS

The first English town in America was built in the Virginia colony in 1607. It was named Jamestown. Captain John Smith was a Jamestown leader. He explored the Potomac River in 1608. Smith was probably the first European to see the land where the capital now stands.

About 1623, English fur trader Henry Fleet came to the D.C. region. Fleet wanted to trade English goods for furs. But the Indians were angry with the English. They had taken the Indians' Virginia lands. The Indians captured Fleet and held him for five years. Fleet became the first European to live in what is now the capital.

Fleet seems to have been well treated by the Indians. He later wrote that the region was "the most pleasant and healthful place in all this country." Fleet added that the woods were filled with "deer, buffaloes, bears, and turkeys."

John Smith was probably the first European to see the Washington, D.C., region.

PLANTERS AND SETTLEMENTS

In 1632, English king Charles I carved the colony of Maryland from Virginia. He gave the new colony to the Calvert family. In 1634, the first colonists

12

came to Maryland. They received large pieces of land from the Calverts. These colonists were called planters. They built plantations, which were large farms. They grew tobacco. Slaves brought from Africa did the work on the plantations.

By the late 1600s, land on both sides of the Potomac River had rich tobacco plantations. Some of this land would become the capital of the United States.

By the mid-1700s, the tobacco trade brought about the need for towns. In 1749, George Washington helped lay out the town of Alexandria, Virginia. At that time, he worked as a surveyor. Alexandria is now just outside of Washington. Georgetown, Maryland, was founded two years later. Today, Georgetown is part of Washington, D.C.

George Washington was working as a surveyor when he helped lay out the town of Alexandria.

THE UNITED STATES FOUNDS A CAPITAL

Besides Virginia and Maryland, England had eleven other American colonies. England ruled these thirteen colonies for many years. Then, from 1775 to 1783, the Americans fought the Revolutionary War. They wanted to be free of England. At first, the Americans didn't seem strong enough to win the war. But George Washington had become the leader of the American army. He led the Americans to victory. The Americans called their new nation the United States of America.

Eight cities served as the United States capital between 1776 and 1790. They were Philadelphia, Pennsylvania; Baltimore, Maryland; Lancaster, Pennsylvania; York, Pennsylvania; Princeton, New Jersey; Annapolis, Maryland; Trenton, New Jersey; and New York, New York. All the moves caused problems. Government papers had to be moved from place to place. Besides, the United States government had to ask the states to protect it.

When Philadelphia was the capital of the United States, the Pennsylvania State House (above) served as the capitol.

In 1783, angry Revolutionary War veterans marched in Philadelphia. They demanded that Congress pay them their back wages from the war. Congress asked Pennsylvania's leaders for help. But the state's leaders refused to supply troops to protect Congress.

In 1787, American leaders made a new framework of government for the nation. It is called the United States Constitution. Among other things, it said that the country should have a permanent capital. Americans argued over where it should be. Finally, the lawmakers decided that the new capital would be on the Potomac River. It also would not

be part of any state. The president would pick the exact spot.

George Washington was serving as the first president. In 1791, Washington chose a spot 15 miles from Mount Vernon. That was the name of his home in Virginia.

At that time, the country had just thirteen states. They were along the East Coast. The new capital would be near their midway point. It would be a good meeting place for lawmakers from around the country. Maryland gave about 70 square miles of land for the new city. Virginia gave 30 square miles, including Alexandria. This land was then owned by the federal government.

Mount Vernon (above) was the Virginia home of President George Washington.

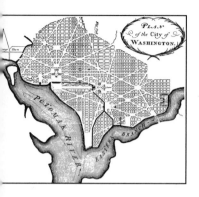

Pierre L'Enfant's plan of the city of Washington

Andrew Ellicott (right) and Benjamin Banneker (left) carried out L'Enfant's plans for the capital city.

President Washington chose Pierre L'Enfant to design the capital. He was a French architect who had fought for America during the Revolutionary War. L'Enfant planned a city with wide streets, public parks, and a long mall. Much of what is seen in the capital today was part of his plan. Surveyors headed by Pennsylvania-born Andrew Ellicott laid out the city's boundaries. Benjamin Banneker worked with Ellicott. He was a black astronomer from Maryland.

Hundreds of workers built the capital during the 1790s. The United States government wanted the city finished by 1800. It wasn't. But that summer, President John Adams moved 130 government workers there from Philadelphia. Congress first met in Washington, D.C., on November 22, 1800. The Congressmen gathered in the unfinished Capitol.

In 1797, John Adams had become the nation's second president. In 1800, John and Abigail Adams became the first couple to live in the "President's Palace." Later, its name was changed to the White House. George Washington never lived there. He died in 1799, two years after retiring as president.

THE YOUNG CAPITAL

The United States Constitution gave Congress complete control of the nation's capital. For the first few years, Washingtonians had no city government. They also could not vote for president. And they weren't represented in Congress, either. The Constitution said that only people who lived in states had those rights. This made Washingtonians very unhappy.

In 1802, Congress set up a city government. The people could vote for a city council. But the president of the United States appointed the city's mayor.

The capital was only a few years old when disaster struck. A war between England and the United States began in 1812. The War of 1812 was fought over control of the seas. In 1814, English forces closed in on the capital.

Benjamin Banneker

President James Madison fled the White House. But First Lady Dolley Madison waited. She didn't leave until the English were very close. She took government papers and a portrait of George Washington with her. She saved these items from being destroyed. For when the English arrived, they burned the White House. The Capitol and other public buildings also went up in flames.

The War of 1812 ended in 1815. That year, work began on restoring the capital. The White House, the Capitol, and the other structures were rebuilt.

In 1820, Congress gave Washingtonians more self-government. The people were allowed to elect their mayor. However, they still couldn't vote for president. They still were not represented in Congress.

The Smithsonian Institution was founded in 1846.

In 1829, an unusual thing happened. James Smithson left $500,000 to the United States government. Smithson was an English scientist. He wanted the government to build a museum with the money. In 1846, Congress founded the Smithsonian Institution. Today, the Smithsonian has fifteen museums and a zoo.

Before 1846, many new buildings had gone up in the capital. This growth occurred north of the

18

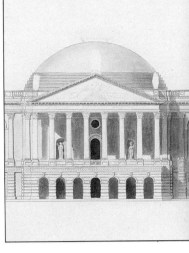

Above: The central portion of William Thornton's winning design for the Capitol Left: The Capitol as it looked in 1846, after the dome had been redesigned by Charles Bulfinch

Potomac. Congress did not think the capital needed its land south of the river. In 1846, Congress gave that land, including Alexandria, back to Virginia. Since then, the capital's basic shape and size haven't changed.

Washington, D.C., had shrunk in size. But its population was growing. By 1850, about fifty-two thousand people lived in the capital. About thirty-eight thousand of them were white. About three thousand were black slaves. About eleven thousand were free black people. Washington had the highest percentage of free blacks of any American city.

Civilian volunteers guarded the White House during the early days of the Civil War.

THE CIVIL WAR

By 1850, slavery was illegal in the northern states. But it was still allowed in the southern states and in D.C. Northerners and southerners had argued over slavery for years. Then, in 1860, Abraham Lincoln was elected president. White southerners feared that he would end slavery.

In 1861, the southern states formed the Confederate States of America (the Confederacy). On April 14, fighting began between the northern states (the Union) and the Confederacy. This was the start of the Civil War (1861-1865). In 1862, Congress outlawed slavery in the capital.

Washington, D.C., was next to Virginia. Virginia fought on the side of the Confederacy. The capital was in danger of being seized by southern troops. In July 1864, a Confederate army reached Silver Spring, Maryland. That was only 6 miles from the capital. The Union rushed troops in. On July 12, the armies fought in Washington. President Lincoln watched from nearby as Union troops drove off the invaders.

The war ended on April 9, 1865. Five days later, President Lincoln and his wife went to a play. The play was at Ford's Theatre, not far from the White House. During the play, John Wilkes Booth shot Lincoln. The president died the next morning. Lincoln was the first president of the United States to be assassinated.

This flyer was issued by the War Department after the assassination of President Abraham Lincoln.

A GOLDEN AGE FOR BLACK WASHINGTONIANS

After the war, Congress worked to make life better for black Americans. In December 1865, the Thirteenth Amendment was passed. It freed all Americans who still were slaves. In 1866, the Fourteenth Amendment gave blacks the rights of American citizens. Also in 1866, Congress granted black men in Washington the right to vote.

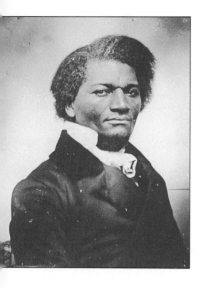

Black leader Frederick Douglass was a Washington official in the 1860s.

Howard University was founded in 1867.

Between 1870 and 1890, the capital's population rose from 130,000 to 230,000. Many of these newcomers were black people. In other cities, white people wouldn't hire blacks. Many blacks in the capital got jobs with the government. Others started their own businesses.

Black Washingtonians achieved a great deal during the late 1800s. In 1867, Howard University was founded. It is a famous mainly black university. Father Patrick Healy, a black priest, was president (1873-1882) of Georgetown University. The great black leader Frederick Douglass worked as an official in D.C. Among other things, he was the United States marshal of the city.

CHANGES AND IMPROVEMENTS

By 1870, the city couldn't meet the needs of its growing population. Some people felt the city needed a new form of government. In 1871, Congress replaced the mayor and council with a territorial government. D.C. then had an appointed governor, Henry D. Cooke. However, the people elected the legislature.

The territory's second governor was Washingtonian Alexander Robey Shepherd. Under him, D.C.'s streets were paved and sidewalks were built. Sewers were laid and trees were planted. The city was much improved. However, within three years, the city owed over $22 million.

In 1874, Congress once again changed Washington's form of government. The president appointed three commissioners to run the city. Washingtonians no longer had home rule. They had lost all self-government.

The capital, however, continued to grow and improve. Telephones were installed in 1877. In the early 1880s, the city received electric lights. The Washington Monument was finished in 1884. In 1897, the first Library of Congress building was

The Library of Congress (left) was completed in 1897. In 1899 (right), these students and their teacher admired the Neptune Fountain in front of the building.

completed. Work began on the Lincoln Memorial in 1914.

By that time, the United States had become a great power. Other nations looked to Washington for answers to world problems.

WORLD WARS AND DEPRESSION

In 1917, the United States entered World War I (1914-1918). The federal government needed more workers for its war offices. About one hundred thousand people came to work in the capital. These people needed homes, schools, and office buildings. The capital had a building boom. In 1918, the United States and its allies won the war.

In 1929, hard times hit the United States. This was called the Great Depression (1929-1939). Millions of Americans lost their jobs, farms, and homes. Thousands of banks failed. People lost their savings.

But in 1933, jobs increased in D.C. In that year, President Franklin D. Roosevelt started the New Deal. New Deal programs helped the United States get out of the depression. The government needed more workers to set up and run these programs. During the New Deal (1933-1939), D.C.'s popula-

tion grew by about 170,000 people. Many of them helped put up new buildings. Work was completed on the Supreme Court Building in 1935. The National Gallery of Art and the Jefferson Memorial were started during the New Deal.

The Great Depression ended with the coming of World War II (1939-1945). The United States entered the war in 1941. Once again, the capital's population grew. The government needed thousands of new workers in its war offices. Washington

The Supreme Court Building was completed in 1935.

25

saw another building boom. In 1944, American and allied diplomats met at Dumbarton Oaks. This is a mansion in Washington. Those diplomats made the first plans for the United Nations (UN). Today, the UN works for world peace in many ways. In 1945, World War II ended. The United States and its allies had won.

CITY OF MARCHES AND PROTESTS

This pebble garden and pool are on the grounds of Dumbarton Oaks, the Washington mansion where plans for the United Nations were begun.

Washington has often been the site of marches and protests. In the 1950s, black Americans were still being mistreated. Black leaders came to the capital to point out many injustices.

In 1957, twenty thousand blacks met in the capital. They came from all around the United

States for the "Prayer Pilgrimage." Dr. Martin Luther King, Jr., spoke at this protest. Six years later, Dr. King led two hundred thousand people in the "March on Washington." The people walked from the Washington Monument to the Lincoln Memorial. There, Dr. King made his famous "I Have a Dream" speech.

Meanwhile, the United States was fighting the Vietnam War (1964-1973) in Southeast Asia. Antiwar people from all over the country went to Washington. They felt the United States should pull out of the war. About fifty thousand antiwar people marched in D.C. in 1967. In 1969, about two hundred thousand marched against the war. Finally, peace talks started. In 1973, the last American troops left Vietnam.

THE FIGHT FOR HOME RULE

During the 1960s, Congress began to listen to many Washington residents' demands for equal political rights. Since 1964, Washingtonians have voted for president. Since 1970, they could send a delegate to the House of Representatives. The delegate cannot vote to pass laws, however. Since 1974, Washingtonians have elected their own mayor and

In many states, blacks were prevented from voting. They were often kept out of good jobs and decent housing. Black children could not attend school with white children.

council. Walter E. Washington was elected in that year. He served until 1979. Then Marion Barry became mayor.

Many Washingtonians view these changes as only a start. The city does not have complete home rule. Congress still must approve major decisions made by the mayor and council. Since the 1980s, there has been a drive to make Washington, D.C., the fifty-first state. In 1982, Washingtonians chose a name for this state. They decided to call it New Columbia. But Congress has not granted statehood.

OTHER RECENT DEVELOPMENTS

Between 1950 and 1990, the D.C. region grew from 1.5 million to 3.9 million people. But this growth took place in the capital's suburbs. These are towns outside of D.C., in Maryland and Virginia. The capital itself has lost people. In fact, its population dipped from 802,178 to 606,900 during those years.

People left Washington for many different reasons. After World War II, more people had cars. Many liked the new, inexpensive houses built outside of the city. Recently, however, people realized that living in the city is very convenient. They are

buying beautiful older homes and fixing them up. This is called renovation.

Like all big cities, Washington has its share of problems with drugs, crime, and poverty. In 1989, the federal government started an $80-million program to fight drugs. Money, though, is not enough. Meeting the challenge, the public schools are teaching self-esteem building and drug-use prevention.

Sharon Pratt Kelly was elected mayor in 1990. She is the city's first woman mayor. Mayor Kelly was born in Washington, D.C., and is a graduate of D.C. public schools. Before her election, she worked as a lawyer and corporation executive. Washingtonians hope that she will lead them in solving their city's problems.

Walter E. Washington (left) served as mayor of D.C. from 1975 to 1979. Mayor Sharon Pratt Kelly (right) was elected in 1990.

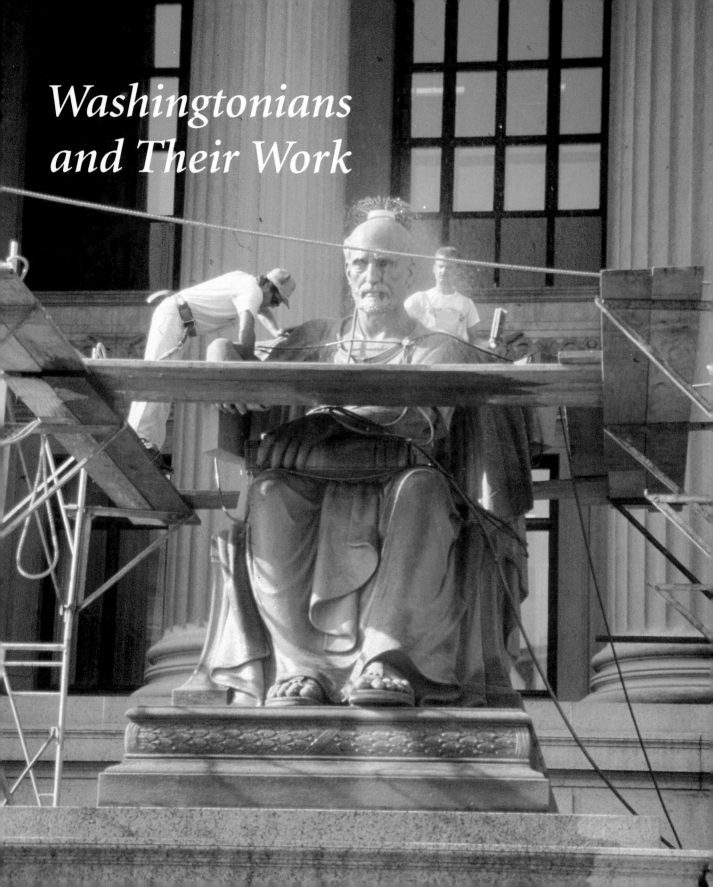

*Washingtonians
and Their Work*

WASHINGTONIANS AND THEIR WORK

To its 606,900 people, Washington, D.C., is more than the United States capital. The city is their home. These people live, work, go to school, and play in Washington.

Two-thirds of all Washingtonians are black. No big American city has a larger percentage of black people. More than a quarter of the city's people are white. One in every twenty is Hispanic. The capital is also home to about eleven thousand Asians. They include people of Chinese, Filipino, and Japanese heritage. In addition, about fifteen hundred American Indians live in the city.

Washington is home to people of nearly every racial, ethnic, and national background.

The nation's paper money is made at the Bureau of Engraving and Printing.

It is widely known that the capital has many poor people. Less known is the fact that it has many rich people. As of 1990, the average income per person was about $24,000. That is one of the highest average incomes of any American city. Washington is the nation's nineteenth-largest city.

The capital differs from other United States cities in another way. Most cities are manufacturing centers. But other than printing and publishing, the capital doesn't have much manufacturing. Each year, a mountain of books, magazines, and pamphlets are produced there. Many of these works come from the Government Printing Office.

National Geographic magazine is also published in Washington.

The United States government is the city's biggest business. About a hundred thousand Washingtonians work for it. That's about a third of the city's workers. Government workers range from the nation's president to the guards at public buildings.

Tourism is the city's second-biggest business. About ten million people visit the capital each year. This provides work for many Washingtonians. Some work in hotels and restaurants. Others run tour services or serve as guides.

Left: Tourists at the House of Representatives
Right: One of the capital's National Park Service guides gives information to a tourist.

A Trip Through
Washington, D.C.

A Trip Through Washington, D.C.

Every American should visit Washington, D.C., at least once. It is thrilling to see the United States Capitol and the White House. It is interesting to watch the nation's government at work.

Capitol Hill

Capitol Hill is a good place to begin a trip through Washington. It rises to a height of 90 feet near the city's center. The Capitol is the most famous building on "the hill." In the Capitol, members of Congress pass laws for the country.

Congress has two houses. One is the Senate. The other is the House of Representatives. Each state elects lawmakers to these two houses. The House of Representatives meets in the world's largest lawmaking chamber. Visitors can watch members of the House and Senate work on laws.

One of the Capitol's 540 rooms is Statuary Hall. The states have placed statues of some of their famous people in the hall. Visitors enjoy finding the statues from their home states.

The Library of Congress (LC) is housed in three buildings near the Capitol. It is the world's largest library. LC has nearly one hundred million books, pictures, and other items.

The Supreme Court Building is a short walk from LC. The Supreme Court is the nation's highest court. Its decisions are very important. All Americans have to live by them.

THE WHITE HOUSE

The White House is the nation's most famous home. More than 1.5 million people visit the White

Left: The west entrance of the Capitol
Right: Statuary Hall, one of the Capitol's 540 rooms

The Red Room, with its portrait of Angelica Van Buren (right), is one of the rooms in the White House (left).

House each year. Tourists can visit 5 of the White House's 132 rooms. They are the Red, Blue, and Green rooms; the East Room; and the State Dining Room. The president holds his press conferences in the East Room.

There are many interesting stories about the White House. Abigail Adams hung the family's laundry in the East Room. President Theodore Roosevelt held wrestling matches in that room. His children roller-skated around the room. President Calvin Coolidge let his pet raccoon, Rebecca, run loose in the White House.

Four Famous Monuments

West of Capitol Hill is a big, grassy parkland called the Mall. Four famous monuments stand on or near the Mall.

One monument is a tall, tapered pillar of marble. This is the Washington Monument. It honors the country's first president. The Washington Monument rises 555 feet into the sky. It is the city's tallest building. Visitors can take an elevator to the top. From there, they can enjoy a great view of the Washington area.

The Lincoln Memorial is directly west of the Washington Monument. It honors the president who saved the nation during the Civil War. Daniel Chester French did the famous statue of Lincoln inside the memorial. Lincoln's Gettysburg Address is carved on an inside wall. The Lincoln Memorial and Washington Monument stand on opposite ends of the Reflecting Pool. The water in the pool reflects the two structures.

There is a picture of the Lincoln Memorial on the backs of United States pennies and five-dollar bills.

The Vietnam Veterans Memorial is a short walk from the Lincoln Memorial. The people of the United States paid for this memorial. It honors the men and women who served in Vietnam. The main part of the memorial is a V-shaped wall. On it are

Maya Lin (above) designed the Vietnam Veterans Memorial.

The Vietnam Veterans Memorial (left) and the Jefferson Memorial (right) are two of Washington's famous monuments.

the names of more than fifty-eight thousand Americans. These people died in Vietnam or remain missing. Maya Ying Lin, a twenty-one-year-old college student, designed the wall.

The Jefferson Memorial stands between the Tidal Basin and the Potomac River. It honors Thomas Jefferson. He was the country's third president. Jefferson was also the author of the Declaration of Independence. There is a statue of Jefferson inside the memorial. Some of his famous writings are carved on the inside walls.

SOME GOVERNMENT BUILDINGS

Most of Washington's important government buildings are not far from the Mall. The Bureau of

Engraving and Printing makes the nation's paper money and stamps. Every day, about $30 million in paper money is printed in this building.

The Federal Bureau of Investigation (FBI) gives exciting tours. The FBI deals with certain major crimes. They include bank robberies, kidnappings, and bombings. FBI agents have tracked down many criminals over the years. On its tours, the FBI shares some of its methods with visitors. The tours end at the shooting range. There, agents go through a target practice.

Not far from the FBI building is the National Archives. Important government papers are stored there for safekeeping. Visitors can see the original Declaration of Independence and Constitution. A few blocks to the northwest is the District Building. This is D.C.'s city hall. The mayor and the city council work in the building. Past leaders of the city's government are honored there.

MUSEUMS ALONG THE MALL

Nine of the Smithsonian Institution's museums are on the north and south sides of the Mall. The National Air and Space Museum is the world's most-visited museum. About eight million people

If all the paper money printed in Washington each year were placed end to end, it would stretch nearly a million miles.

The National Archives

41

Two of the Smithsonian Institution's museums are the National Air and Space Museum (left) and the National Museum of Natural History (right).

go there yearly. One of its exhibits is the Flyer. In 1903, the Wright brothers made the first airplane flight with that machine. The National Museum of Natural History has dinosaur skeletons. It also has exhibits on American Indians. The National Museum of American History has a famous 50-foot flag. Watching this flag inspired Francis Scott Key to write "The Star-Spangled Banner."

The Smithsonian has several art museums. The National Museum of African Art displays ancient and modern African artworks. The National Gallery of Art has famous American and European paintings. About a half mile north of the Mall is the National Portrait Gallery. It has pictures of famous Americans.

Other Smithsonian museums and a zoo are in other parts of Washington. Altogether, the Smithsonian Institution now owns almost 140 million objects. That's why the Smithsonian is called "the nation's attic." It would take one person about 265 years to view everything.

NEIGHBORHOODS IN NORTHWEST D.C.

Washington, D.C., has rich, poor, and average neighborhoods. One of the richest ones is Georgetown. It is in the far western part of Northwest D.C. Georgetown has many lovely homes that were built in the 1700s.

Georgetown is a neighborhood in Northwest D.C.

This part of Washington is also home to Georgetown University. Founded in 1789, it is the country's oldest Catholic university. It has had many great basketball teams. In 1984, Georgetown University won the national college basketball championship.

East of Georgetown is a neighborhood called Foggy Bottom. This area was once a foggy swamp along the Potomac River. In the 1800s, many factories operated in the neighborhood. They put forth smoke and steam. In that way, the factories added to the name "Foggy Bottom."

43

The Kennedy Center is named in memory of President John F. Kennedy. Kennedy was assassinated in Dallas, Texas, on November 22, 1963.

Today, Foggy Bottom is a neighborhood for the arts and learning. The John F. Kennedy Center for the Performing Arts is there. Plays, dance programs, operas, and concerts are performed in the building. George Washington University is also in Foggy Bottom.

About a mile north of Foggy Bottom is Embassy Row. The embassies of about one hundred countries line Massachusetts Avenue and nearby streets. Each country flies its flag outside its embassy. Officials from foreign governments work in the embassies. They work to keep good relations with the United States.

North of Embassy Row is the National Zoo. It is part of the Smithsonian Institution. The zoo is

A boa constrictor at the National Zoo's petting zoo

home to giant pandas and great apes. Hundreds of other kinds of animals are also found there.

East of the zoo is the Adams-Morgan neighborhood. It has been called D.C.'s "United Nations." People from Africa, Southeast Asia, and Latin America live there.

East of Adams-Morgan is one of Washington's oldest black neighborhoods. Howard University is in the center of it. Howard was founded in 1867 for black people. Today, it is one of the country's largest mainly black universities.

SIGHTS IN NORTHEAST AND SOUTHEAST D.C.

Northeast D.C. is the home of Gallaudet College. Gallaudet is a school for deaf students. All classes there are taught through sign language.

East of Gallaudet is the National Arboretum. All kinds of trees and plants are studied there. East, across the Anacostia River, is Kenilworth Aquatic Gardens. Water plants such as lilies and bamboo are grown in its waters.

To the south, on the west bank of the Anacostia, stands RFK Stadium. The Washington Redskins, D.C.'s pro football team, play there. They won the Super Bowl in 1983, 1988, and 1992.

The Washington Redskins won Super Bowl XXII in 1988 (above).

RFK Stadium was named in memory of Senator Robert F. Kennedy. Kennedy was assassinated in Los Angeles, California, on June 5, 1968, while campaigning to be president of the United States.

Southeast Washington is made up mainly of houses, apartments, and small stores. One of its neighborhoods is Anacostia. It lies along the southeast bank of the Anacostia River. Many freed slaves settled there right after the Civil War. Cedar Hill, the home of Frederick Douglass, is in the neighborhood. The Anacostia Museum, part of the Smithsonian, is also there. This museum shows the history and culture of African Americans.

NEARBY HIGHLIGHTS

Some places in Virginia and Maryland are part of the D.C. area. The Pentagon is in Arlington, Virginia. That is across the Potomac River from Washington. This five-sided structure is the world's largest office building. The Pentagon is the headquarters of the Department of Defense. The main offices of the United States Army, Navy, Air Force, and Coast Guard are there.

Arlington National Cemetery is near the Pentagon. Nearly two hundred thousand American soldiers are buried there. Some of them fought in the Revolutionary War. The Tomb of the Unknowns is in the cemetery. It contains the bodies of four United States soldiers who couldn't be iden-

More than twenty-five thousand people work in the Pentagon. It is the world's largest office building.

tified. All dead American soldiers whose names are unknown are honored by this memorial. The graves of John and Robert Kennedy have special places in the cemetery.

Mount Vernon, George Washington's home, is a more cheerful place to visit. It is in Virginia, 15 miles south of D.C. Visitors can see Washington's bed and many of his belongings.

Many D.C. sports fans travel to Largo, Maryland. There, about 4 miles from Washington, is the Capital Centre. D.C.'s pro basketball and hockey teams play there. The Washington Bullets won the National Basketball. Association (NBA) championship in 1978. The Washington Capitals—called the Caps—are D.C.'s pro hockey team.

A memorial to the astronauts who died in the space shuttle Challenger *disaster (right) stands in Arlington National Cemetery (left).*

A Gallery of Famous Washingtonians

A GALLERY OF FAMOUS WASHINGTONIANS

More famous people have worked in the nation's capital than in any other American city. Most of them were born elsewhere, however. The following people were all born in Washington, D.C.

From his childhood, **John Philip Sousa** (1854-1932) loved music. He studied the violin and trombone. Then he joined the U.S. Marine Band in the capital. Sousa became its conductor in 1880. He wrote marches for the band. His pieces were so popular that he was nicknamed the "March King." Sousa's marches include "The Stars and Stripes Forever" and "The Washington Post." He also wrote the Marines' Hymn ("Semper Fidelis").

Charles Drew (1904-1950) went to Washington's Dunbar High School. He then attended college and became a famous doctor. In 1940, Drew found ways to store blood. He then helped set up blood banks in the United States and England. Dr. Drew's work saved millions of lives during and since World War II. Drew also taught at Howard University. There, he trained many black doctors.

John Philip Sousa

J. Edgar Hoover

Benjamin O. Davis (left) was the first black U. S. army general. His son, Benjamin O. Davis, Jr. (right), was the first black U. S. Air Force general.

J. Edgar Hoover (1895-1972) started working for the government after high school graduation. He was a messenger for the Library of Congress. He also studied law at night at George Washington University. Hoover became a lawyer and an expert on crime. In 1924, he was made director of the Bureau of Investigation. In 1935, it became the FBI. Hoover held the post until his death forty-eight years later. The FBI building in D.C. was named in his honor—the J. Edgar Hoover Building.

John Foster Dulles (1888-1959) also earned his law degree from George Washington University. Dulles became a diplomat. He dealt with other nations for his government. In 1945, he helped found the United Nations (UN). The UN works for world peace. In 1951, Dulles worked out a peace treaty with Japan. From 1953 until just before his death, Dulles was the U.S. secretary of state.

Benjamin O. Davis (1877-1970) and his son **Benjamin O. Davis, Jr.** (born in 1912), had much in

common besides their names. Both achieved military "firsts." In 1940, Benjamin O. Davis became the first black U.S. Army general. In 1954, Benjamin O. Davis, Jr., became the U.S. Air Force's first black general.

Several black Washingtonians have also achieved political "firsts." In 1966, **Robert Weaver** (born in 1907) became secretary of the U.S. Department of Housing and Urban Development (HUD). He was the first black member of a president's cabinet. **Edward Brooke** (born in 1919) was elected to the U.S. Senate from Massachusetts in 1966. Brooke was the first black person elected to the U.S. Senate in about a hundred years.

Marjorie Kinnan Rawlings (1896-1953) was one of the best writers born in D.C. Her novel *The Yearling* won a Pulitzer Prize in 1939. Playwright **Edward Albee** was born in 1928. His works include *Who's Afraid of Virginia Woolf?* and *The Zoo Story*. He won the Pulitzer Prize in 1967 and 1975 for other plays.

Carl Bernstein (born in 1944) is a famous newspaper reporter. While working for the *Washington Post,* Bernstein helped uncover the Watergate scandal. In 1972, White House-backed burglars broke into Democratic party headquarters.

Marjorie Kinnan Rawlings

Carl Bernstein

Connie Chung

Adrian Dantley

Those offices were in the Watergate Building. In 1974, President Richard Nixon resigned because of this scandal. Television newscasters **Connie Chung** (born in 1946) and **Roger Mudd** (born in 1928) are also D.C. natives.

Washington, D.C., has also produced some great athletes. They include basketball stars **Elgin Baylor** (born in 1934) and **Adrian Dantley** (born in 1956). Baylor averaged 27.4 points per game during his fourteen-year pro career. He played with both the Minneapolis and Los Angeles Lakers. Only Michael Jordan and Wilt Chamberlain have higher game averages. Dantley won the NBA scoring crown twice during the 1980s. **Maury Wills** (born in 1932) was a great baseball player. In 1962, Wills was the National League's Most Valuable Player. He was a star with the Los Angeles Dodgers.

Jazz great **Duke Ellington** (1899-1974) was one of the best entertainers from Washington. Ellington led his own jazz band. He wrote songs such as "Don't Get Around Much Anymore" and "Sophisticated Lady." The Academy Award-winning actresses **Helen Hayes** (1900-1993) and **Goldie Hawn** (born in 1945) are also D.C. natives. Another actress from D.C. must be mentioned. Her name was **Billie Burke** (1885-1970). She is best

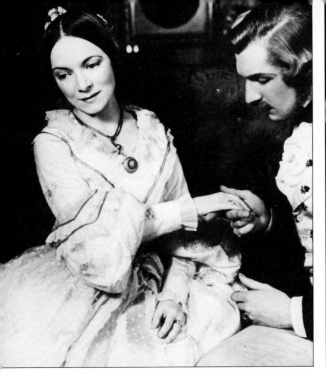 

remembered for her role in *The Wizard of Oz*. She played Glinda, the good witch.

Helen Hayes (left) and Billie Burke (right) are two famous actresses who were born in D.C.

The birthplace of many famous people including Dr. Charles Drew, John Philip Sousa, J. Edgar Hoover, and Billie Burke . . .

The place that George Washington chose for the United States capital and that was then named for him . . .

The site of the White House, the Capitol, the Washington Monument, and the Lincoln Memorial . . .

The city where laws for the United States are made and the country's money is printed . . .

This is Washington, D.C.—the nation's capital!

Did You Know?

In 1962, at the age of four, Dorothy Straight of Washington, D.C., wrote a book called *How the World Began*. Two years later, it was published.

Each spring, the Cherry Blossom Festival is held in D.C. At that time, the Japanese cherry trees that ring the Tidal Basin are in full bloom.

The United States would have to design a new fifty-one-star flag if Washington, D.C., became a state.

Twenty-six inches of snow fell on the capital on January 27-29, 1922. The snow collapsed the roof of the Knickerbocker Theater, killing 98 people.

One of the largest flags ever made, "The Great American Flag," was displayed at the Washington Monument in 1981. It measures 411 feet by 210 feet—much larger than a football field.

John Quincy Adams and Theodore Roosevelt enjoyed swimming in the Potomac River while they were president.

President Warren G. Harding liked to practice his golf game on the White House lawn. Laddie Boy, his dog, retrieved the balls.

In 1921, Margaret Gorman of Washington, D.C., was the first Miss America. Venus Ramey of D.C. was Miss America for 1924.

A picture of the White House can be seen on the backs of twenty-dollar bills.

If it achieves statehood, Washington, D.C., will be the smallest state. Washington is one-eighteenth the size of Rhode Island, which is now the smallest state.

Quite a few Washingtonians have the same names as former presidents. The 1991-1992 D.C. phone book lists ten men named John Adams; five each named George Washington and John Kennedy; three each named James Monroe, Andrew Jackson, John Tyler, and James Polk; and one each named Thomas Jefferson, William H. Harrison, James Buchanan, Andrew Johnson, Benjamin Harrison, William McKinley, William Taft, Woodrow Wilson, and Jimmy Carter.

Washingtonians elected Jesse Jackson as their "shadow senator" in 1990. He cannot sit in the Senate or vote there. His job is working for D.C.'s statehood.

For one hundred years (1874-1974), it required an Act of Congress to do just about anything in D.C.—even to get a dog license!

Walter Johnson of the Washington Senators was one of the fastest pitchers who ever lived. The "Big Train," as he was called, won 416 games with the Senators over his twenty-one year career.

James Smithson, the English scientist who founded the Smithsonian Institution, never visited the United States. But his tomb is in the Smithsonian's first building—the Castle.

WASHINGTON, D.C., INFORMATION

The D.C. flag

American beauty rose

Wood thrush

Area: 69 square miles

Borders: Maryland on the northwest, northeast, and southeast; Virginia on the southwest across the Potomac River

Highest Point: 410 feet above sea level, in Northwest D.C.

Lowest Point: 1 foot above sea level, along the Potomac River

Hottest Recorded Temperature: 106° F., on July 30, 1930

Coldest Recorded Temperature: -15° F., on February 11, 1899

Date of Founding: George Washington chose the site in 1791; the city became the U.S. capital in 1800

Origin of Name: The city was named in honor of George Washington; Columbia is a nickname for the United States that honors explorer Christopher Columbus

City Motto: *Justitia Omnibus* (Latin, meaning "Justice for all")

Nicknames: "Nation's Capital," "Capital City"

City Seal: Adopted in 1871

City Flag: Adopted in 1938

City Flower: American beauty rose

City Bird: Wood thrush

Rivers: Potomac, Anacostia

Wildlife: Squirrels, rabbits, raccoons, foxes, opossums, muskrats, warblers, Baltimore orioles, chickadees, many other kinds of birds.

Economy: Government work, tourism, printing, publishing, construction work

Population: 606,900, nineteenth-largest U.S. city (1990 U.S. Census Bureau figures)

Population of Metropolitan Area (D.C. and its suburbs in Maryland and Virginia): 3,900,000

WASHINGTON, D.C., HISTORY

2000 B.C.—Ancient Indians first reach the Washington, D.C., region

1608—Captain John Smith reaches the site of the future Washington, D.C.

1623—Henry Fleet becomes the first European to live in the Washington, D.C., region

1749—George Washington helps lay out Alexandria, Virginia

1751—Georgetown is organized as a town

1775—The Revolutionary War begins

1776—The Declaration of Independence announces the birth of the United States

1783—The Americans win the Revolutionary War; Revolutionary War veterans demand that Congress pay their back wages

1787—The U.S. Constitution gives Congress authority over the land that will become the nation's capital

1791—George Washington chooses the site of Washington, D.C., as the nation's capital

1800—John Adams moves the federal government from Philadelphia to Washington, D.C.; the Adamses become the first family to live in the White House; D.C.'s population is about 14,000

1802—Congress allows Washingtonians to elect a city council; the president appoints the mayor

1814—The British burn the White House, the Capitol, and other public buildings during the War of 1812

1820—Congress allows Washingtonians to elect their mayors

1846—Part of the capital's land, including Alexandria, is returned to Virginia; the Smithsonian Institution is founded

1850—The capital's population reaches almost 52,000

1861—The Civil War begins

The British burned the capital during the War of 1812.

The White House as it looked in 1877

1862—Congress frees the slaves in D.C.

1864—The capital is saved when Union troops fight off the Confederates on July 12

1865—The Civil War ends on April 9; President Abraham Lincoln is assassinated on April 14

1866—Black men in D.C. are given the right to vote

1867—Howard University is founded

1871—Congress ends Washington's mayor-city council government and sets up a territorial government

1874—Congress ends the territorial government and allows the president to appoint commissioners to run the city

1881—President James Garfield is shot in a D.C. railroad station; he dies eleven weeks later in New Jersey

1884—The Washington Monument is completed

1900—The population of D.C. reaches almost 279,000

1914—Work begins on the Lincoln Memorial

1917-1918—About 5,000 black Washingtonians help the United States and its allies win World War I; the city's population increases by about 100,000

1929—The Great Depression begins in the United States

1933-1939—President Franklin D. Roosevelt's New Deal programs help ease the depression; the city's population increases by about 170,000

1941-1945—The United States and its allies fight and win World War II; the city's population increases by more than 100,000

1961—Washingtonians gain the right to vote for the president and vice-president of the United States

1963—Dr. Martin Luther King, Jr., makes his famous "I Have a Dream" speech during the March on Washington

1964—Washingtonians vote for president and vice-president for the first time

1967—D.C.'s commissioner government ends; President Lyndon B Johnson appoints a mayor and a city council

1970—Congress allows Washingtonians to elect a nonvoting delegate to the House of Representatives

1973—Congress allows Washingtonians to elect their mayor and city council

1982—Washingtonians draw up a constitution to make their city the fifty-first state

1990—D.C.'s population is 606,900; Sharon Pratt Dixon (later to become Sharon Pratt Kelly) is elected mayor

1991—The two-hundredth anniversary of the selection of Washington, D.C., as the nation's capital is observed

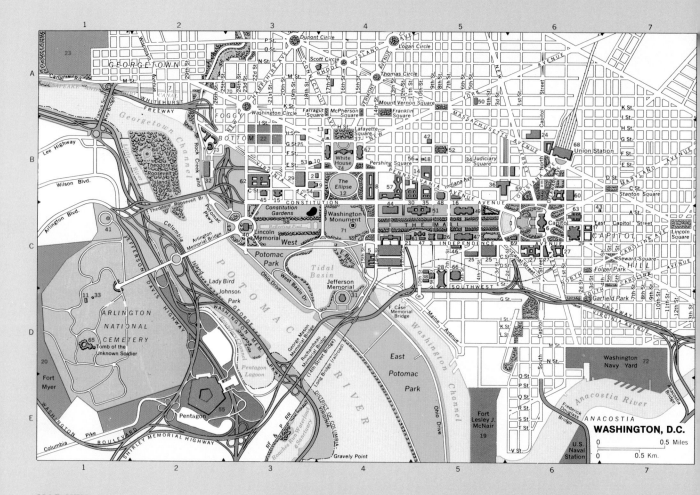

WASHINGTON, D.C.

0   0.5 Miles

0   0.5 Km.

MAP KEY

1. Agriculture, Department of	C4
2. American Red Cross Headquarters	B3
3. Arts and Industries Building	C5
4. Blair House	B4
5. Bureau of Engraving and Printing	C4
6. Capitol	C6
7. Chesapeake and Ohio Canal	A2
8. Commerce, Department of	B4
9. Constitution Hall	B4
10. Corcoran Gallery of Art	B4
11. Custis-Lee Mansion (Arlington House)	D1
12. Ellipse	B4
13. Executive Office Building	B3
14. Federal Bureau of Investigation (J. Edgar Hoover Building)	B5
15. Federal Reserve Board	B3
16. Federal Trade Commission	B5
17. Folger Shakespeare Library	C6
18. Ford's Theatre	B5
19. Fort Lesley J. McNair	E5
20. Fort Meyer	D1
21. Freer Gallery of Art	C4
22. George Washington University	B3
23. Georgetown University	A1
24. Government Printing Office	B6
25. Health and Human Services, Department of	C5
26. Hirshhorn Museum and Sculpture Garden	C5
27. House Office Buildings	C6
28. Housing and Urban Development, Department of	C5
29. Interior, Department of the	B3
30. Internal Revenue Building	B4
31. Jefferson Memorial	D4
32. John F. Kennedy Center for the Performing Arts	B2
33. John F. Kennedy Eternal Flame	D1
34. Judiciary Square	B5
35. Justice, Department of	B5
36. Labor, Department of	B5
37. Lafayette Square	B4
38. L'Enfant Plaza	C5
39. Library of Congress	C6
40. Lincoln Memorial	C3
41. Marine Corps War Memorial	C1
42. Martin Luther King Memorial Library	B5
43. Museum of African Art	C6
44. Museum of American History, National	C4
45. National Academy of Sciences	B3
46. National Aeronautics and Space Administration	C5
47. National Air and Space Museum	C5
48. National Archives	B5
49. National Gallery of Art	C5
50. National Historical Wax Museum	A5
51. National Museum of Natural History	C4
52. National Portrait Gallery	B5
53. Octagon House	B3
54. Organization of American States	B4
55. Pentagon (Department of Defense)	E2
56. Petersen House	B4
57. Postal Service	B4
58. Reflecting Pool	C3
59. Robert A. Taft Memorial	B6
60. Senate Office Buildings	B6
61. Smithsonian Institution Building	C4
62. State, Department of	B3
63. Supreme Court	B6
64. Theodore Roosevelt Memorial	B2
65. Tomb of the Unknowns	D1
66. Transportation, Department of	C5
67. Treasury Building	B4
68. Union Station	B6
69. United States Botanic Garden	C6
70. United States Weather Bureau	A3
71. Washington Monument	C4
72. Washington Navy Yard	D7
73. Watergate Complex	B2
74. White House	B4
75. World Bank	B3

GLOSSARY

allies: Nations that help one another, especially during a war

amendment: A change made in the U.S. Constitution

ancestor: A person from whom one is descended, such as a grandfather or a great-grandmother

ancient: Relating to those living at a time early in history

architect: A person who designs buildings

assassinate: To murder someone who is in politics or government, usually by a secret or sudden attack

astronomer: A person who studies the stars, the planets, and other heavenly bodies

blood banks: Places where blood is stored

cabinet: The president's main advisors

capital: A city that is the seat of government

Capitol (U.S.): The building where Congress meets

climate: The typical weather of a region

colony: A settlement outside a parent country and ruled by the parent country

commissioner: A government official who is appointed to run a district

council: The lawmaking body for a city

diplomat: A person who deals with the governments of other nations for his or her own government

district: An area or region that is governed in a special way

embassies: Buildings where officials representing foreign governments have their headquarters

exhibit: A collection of objects displayed for viewing in places such as museums

federal: Anything related to the government of the United States based in Washington, D.C.

fossils: Remains of animals or plants that lived long ago

headquarters: The place where decisions are made

legislature: A lawmaking body of a state, territory, or nation

manufacturing: The making of products

marshal: A kind of law enforcement officer

million: A thousand thousand (1,000,000)

moccasin: Soft shoes made of animal skins

pilgrimage: A journey made for a religious purpose or another important reason

population: The number of people in a place

prehistoric: Belonging to the time before written history

sign language: A silent language for deaf people that is done by hand and finger movements

suburbs: Towns or villages that develop near large cities

surveyor: A person who measures land boundaries

territory: A region owned or controlled by another government

tourism: The business of providing such services as food and lodging for travelers

INDEX

Page numbers in boldface type indicate illustrations.

ABOUT THE AUTHOR

Dennis Brindell Fradin is the author of 150 published children's books. His works for Childrens Press include the Young People's Stories of Our States series, the Disaster! series, and the Thirteen Colonies series. Dennis is married to Judith Bloom Fradin, who taught high-school and college English for many years. She is now Dennis's chief researcher. The Fradins are the parents of two sons, Anthony and Michael, and a daughter, Diana. Dennis graduated from Northwestern University in 1967 with a B.A. in creative writing, and has lived in Evanston, Illinois, since that year.